GW01218114

BIG
FISH

Written by Steve Parker
Illustrated by Steve Johnson

Henderson Publishing

Woodbridge, England

GENTLE GIANTS

What's the BIGGEST fish in the world?

It's the truck-sized whale shark. This rare beast is the longest and heaviest fish alive today.

It cruises in the surface waters of the sea, with its vast mouth wide open, eating plankton (tiny floating plants and animals).

It's greenish-grey with white spots, and it grows to....

Hold on! Is it a shark or a whale?

Although the whale shark is named after a whale, because it is so big, it is a proper fish, a member of the shark group of fishes.

Anyway, the whale shark grows to . .

But what's the difference?

Do you mean: What is a true fish? A nature expert would say that a fish is a cold-blooded animal with a backbone and skeleton inside, scales outside, fins and a tail for swimming, and gills for breathing.

Where do fish live?

Nearly all fish live in water. Almost any body of water has fish in it - from a tiny stream to a big river, from a little pond to a large lake, from a seashore rockpool to the open ocean, to the darkest depths of the sea.

As we were saying, the whale shark grows to . .

How about seahorses and eels? Are they fish?

Yes, they are. In fact, recognizing a true fish is not so simple.

• Some fish have tiny scales or none at all, like catfishes and leather carp.

• Some can live and breathe out of water for a time, like mudskippers.

• Some have very small or no fins, like eels and lampreys.

• Some are very different from the usual fish shape, such as the strange seahorses, flatfishes and rays.

So beware! All these, along with thousands of others, from sharks to cod, goldfish to sticklebacks, most certainly are fish!

Well, what are *not* fish?

Many creatures live in water, but they aren't fish. There are whales and dolphins, as mentioned before, and seals and sea lions. All of these are warm-blooded mammals, like us.

Sea snakes and sea turtles are reptiles, like snakes and tortoises on land. There are also swimming seabirds, such as penguins and razorbills.

None of these has gills. They all breathe air into their lungs.

What about a jellyfish or starfish?

No, they aren't fish, either. There are many creatures with "fish" in their names, but they aren't true fish. Jellyfish and starfish are two examples. They don't have a backbone, or scales, or fins.

So how many kinds of fish are there?

There are about 22,000 different types, or species, of fish. Most of them are between 10 and 30 centimetres (4 and 12 inches) long. So any fish bigger than you is something of a giant in the fish world.

Can you think of other "fish" that aren't really fish? What about a crayfish, or a crawfish, or the various kinds of shellfish?

Being very big is a way of avoiding being eaten. In fact many of the biggest fish are peaceful creatures, that feed on the tiniest animals and plants in the sea.

OK. After all that, how big is a whale shark?

The largest whale shark ever seen close-to was about 17 metres (55 feet) long, and probably weighed around 35 tonnes*. That's the same as seven full-grown African elephants! It got stuck in a fish trap in Thailand, in 1919.

The biggest whale shark carefully measured by scientists was 12.6 metres (41 feet) long, and weighed about 21 tonnes. It was caught near Pakistan in 1949.

(* One tonne in the metric system is almost the same as one ton in the old imperial system.)

Home of the giants

Whale sharks are found in warm waters around the world, in the central Pacific, Atlantic and Indian Oceans. They rarely go into cooler waters like those around Britain. The farthest north a whale shark has been trapped or caught is North Carolina, USA.

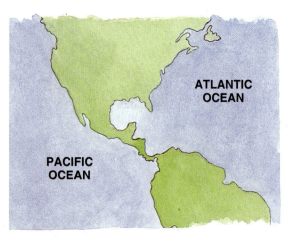

ATLANTIC OCEAN

PACIFIC OCEAN

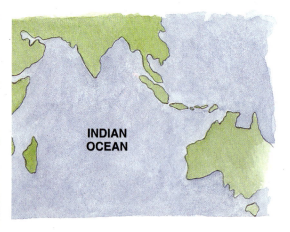

INDIAN OCEAN

Problems measuring fish

Because fish live in the water and rarely stay still, they are difficult for us to measure. Swimming around, half-hidden, they often look much bigger than they really are. Only if they are caught, or if they have just died, can they be weighed and measured accurately. And only if there is a huge pair of weighing scales and a tape measure at hand.

Claims for big fish

This is why there have been many amazing claims by people who think they have seen even bigger whale sharks. One whale shark from near Honduras, Central America, may have been 20 metres (65 feet) long.

Another whale shark, nicknamed "Big Ben" from Mexican waters, was thought to be nearly 23 metres (75 feet) long. This is as huge as a juggernaut container-truck!

How long is 17 metres?

You can measure 17 metres with a tape measure, if you can find one long enough and a room big enough! Many school classrooms are too small. You may have to go into a hall or outside.

If you haven't got a tape measure, get 12 or 13 average 10-year-old children. Ask them to lie down in a long row, head-to-heels. That's about 17 metres!

The meaning of "big"

Normally, what we mean by the "biggest" animal of some kind, is the greatest weight. Some creatures can be extremely long, yet thin and light. So weight is usually the most important dimension, not length or width.

Fish versus whale

How does the whale shark compare with a real whale? It's quite a lot smaller. Even "Big Ben", if it really was 23 metres (75 feet) in length, would be 10 metres shorter than the longest-ever blue whale.

In fact, "Big Ben" was probably a she, because in most fish, the females grow bigger than the males of their kind.

Fat shark

The whale shark is very tubby, as sharks go. One huge specimen measured 7 metres (23 feet) around the fattest part of its body, near the front fins and gill slits. Get five 10-year-old children to lie down head-to-heels in a circle. This is how wide the whale shark can grow!

The biggest animal of all

In fact, blue whales are the longest and heaviest animals of all time. At 35 tonnes, a whale shark still weighs only one-third of an average big blue whale.

One gigantic female blue whale, caught by whalers in 1947, was supposed to weigh 190 tonnes.
That's over five times as much as a whale shark!

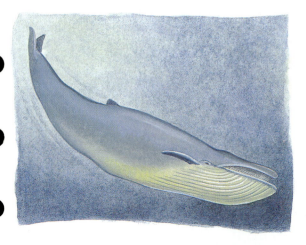

Almost the biggest

The basking shark is the second biggest fish in the world. Like the whale shark, it is a filter feeder, sieving tiny plants and creatures from near the surface. It moves quite slowly and it looks like it is sunbathing or basking in the sun, hence its name.

How big's the basker?

The basking shark is thought to grow to a bus-sized 14 metres (46 feet) long. But the longest reliable measurement was 12.3 metres (40 feet). This animal weighed about 16 tonnes. It got caught in a herring net in the Bay of Fundy, Canada, over 140 years ago!

Other basking sharks

Basking sharks live in temperate (cooler) waters, mainly in the North Atlantic Ocean. They are sometimes seen around Britain. The basking shark is slimmer than the whale shark, and so it weighs less for its length. A few baskers over 11 metres long have been caught, but the average size is probably 8 metres (26 feet) in length and about 5 tonnes in weight.

Megamouth

On the 15 November 1976, near the islands of Hawaii in the Pacific Ocean, some deep-sea fishermen caught a huge, strange-looking shark. Its great gaping mouth, full of tiny teeth, glowed in the dark! No one had ever seen anything like it. In fact, it was a new discovery - a fish unknown to fish experts. It was christened the megamouth shark. It is thought that these wide-mouthed monsters live in deep water, where they filter small creatures from the sea.

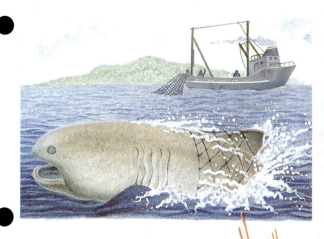

At-an-angle fish

The rare, ribbon-shaped oarfish normally swims at an angle of 45 degrees, with its flowing "mane" streaming out behind it. The pelvic (lower rear) fins are held out in front, to detect the tiny shrimps on which it feeds.

Black shadow

Manta rays are also known as "devil fish".

Good food guides

The strange flaps on either side of the manta's head are food guides. They guide small bits of food into its mouth as it cruises along. For, like the huge sharks and the great whales, the manta ray is a plankton-feeder. You could fit through its mouth sideways!

The original sea-serpent?

The oarfish is one of the longest of all fish. It may be the creature which started legends of great

They are members of the ray group, closely related to sharks. A big manta ray has a "wingspan", across its pectoral (side) fins, of more than 6 metres (20 feet). Despite its great weight of 1,600 kilograms (3,500 pounds), it is a graceful and agile swimmer, able to jump almost clear out of the water.

sea snakes and sea serpents.
The longest one measured properly was 6.4 metres (21 feet).

Jaws!

The great white shark is the largest meat-eating fish in the world. These monsters of modern films have terrified people for centuries.

In 1758 a great white shark was caught, and it contained the headless body of a man in a suit of armour!

Unfussy feeder

The great white shark is also called the white death shark, the blue pointer or the white pointer. And it is known as the "maneater" - although it eats women and children too!

Biggest maneaters

The largest great whites ever seen were probably about 9.5 metres (31 feet) in length. The great white can be very wide too, especially the females, and weigh well over 2,000 kilograms (2 tonnes).

The longest scientifically measured great white shark was 6.4 metres (21 feet). She was also the heaviest, at 3,312 kilograms (7,302 pounds). That's equal to the weight of about 100 average 10-year-old children!

Biggest bite
The bite left by a big great white shark is almost 80 centimetres (30 inches) wide. Its dozens of teeth are 75 millimetres (3 inches) long. They can squeeze with a crushing force of 50 tonnes per square inch!

Tiger of the sea
The great white may be the biggest meat-eater in the ocean, but the tiger shark is one of the fiercest and most dangerous sharks. The tiger grows up to 6 metres (nearly 20 feet) long. Beware when this terrifying creature is hungry. It is not a fussy about its diet and will eat anything it can swallow - paint cans, coal, cigarette packets, shoes, dogs, sheep, and pieces of human!

The hammerhead
The great hammerhead shark grows to 5 metres (over 16 feet) long. Its strange hammer-shaped head probably helps it to see better, and to detect its victims by the tiny electrical signals that their body muscles send out through the water. The hammerhead feeds on rays hiding buried on the sea bottom. But it will attack humans. Divers know it as one of the most unpredictable of the big killers.

Beach danger

Bullsharks live around the South African coast. They grow to 3.5 metres (almost 12 feet) in length. They are dangerous because of their habit of hanging around beaches and estuaries (river mouths), where people swim. They even swim up rivers into lakes.

Fair warning

The grey reef shark is only 2.5 metres (8 feet) long, and it lives in the Pacific Ocean. It does a "dance" before it attacks, weaving and rolling with its back arched. It likes to defend its own patch of reef, and it warns divers to keep away by its dance.

Lazy killer

The sand tiger shark is a sluggish creature of warm Atlantic coastal waters. It spends most of its time dozing on the seabed, until it is hungry. Then it heads for shallow water and feeds voraciously on anything it can catch, even swimmers. It has little trouble swallowing a full-grown person, since it grows to 6 metres (20 feet) long.

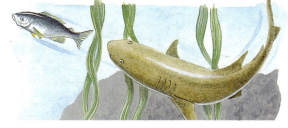

Blue whaler

The great blue shark is about 5 metres (over 16 feet) long. It spends its time cruising lazily near the surface, its dorsal (back) fin sticking above the water in true shark fashion. This shark usually feeds on fish such as mackerel. But when it smells blood, especially from a whaling ship, it goes crazy. It attacks the dead whale bodies in a feeding frenzy, and tries to bite any sailor who attempts to beat it off.

Fast and furious

Barracuda are sleek fish up to 2 metres (6.5 feet) long, and they swim fast through tropical waters. They are vicious predators of smaller fish, and there are several reports of barracudas attacking bathers or divers. These predators lurk in shallow water with their huge, pike-like teeth at the ready. They are not sharks, but members of the large perch fish group.

Once bitten . . .

The moray eels are the biggest eels. A typical big moray hides most of its 3 metres (10 feet) of wriggly, snake-like body in a rock crevice, with only its head showing. It may bite divers that come too close,

because it mistakes them for its favourite food - octopus!
Once the moray bites, it rarely lets go. A diver held fast can risk running out of air! With their bright colours and dramatic patterns, morays are relatively common fish.

Down to the bone

South American piranhas are freshwater fish, and only 40 centimetres (16 inches) long. But they have a giant reputation. They live in big shoals and have mouths shaped like razor-sharp "beaks". When an animal or a person falls into their river, the piranhas follow the scent and go crazy. In a feeding frenzy they can strip the flesh off the victim in seconds, leaving just the bones.

Grouper stalker

Giant Queensland groupers, of the Great Barrier Reef near Australia, grow up to 3 metres (almost 10 feet) in length and weigh over 500 kilograms (1,100 pounds).These fish, also called grupers or gropers, have hearty appetites and huge mouths full of teeth. There are stories of a giant grouper stalking a skin diver, like a cat stalking a mouse - and even swallowing a diver whole!

Hand-feeding the monster

But grouper attacks seem unlikely. Some giant groupers at the reef's tourist areas have become so tame, that skin-diving holidaymakers feed them titbits by hand!

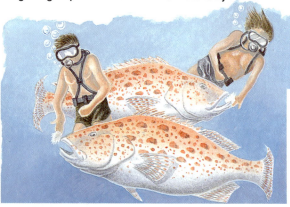

STREAMLINED KILLERS

Lethal weapon
Swordfish are huge hunters of the open ocean. They can reach almost 5 metres (over 16 feet) in length, including at least a metre of spear-like sword, and they weigh up to 680 kilograms (1,500 pounds).

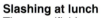

Longest fight
The massive, muscular black marlin is one of the most prized game fishes. It has tremendous fighting power. Near New Zealand in 1968, a black marlin fought the fisherman who hooked it for over 32 hours - then it broke free!

Big marlins
The black marlin is the largest of the marlin group. The biggest caught by rod and line was 707 kilograms (1,560 pounds) in weight, and approaching 6 metres (20 feet) long.

Slashing at lunch
The swordfish's streamlined shape and powerful, sickle-shaped thrashing tail thrust it through the water at great speed. These hunters charge into shoals of fish, striking with their swords and eating whatever they can catch.

A great trophy

The next biggest marlin is the blue marlin, which attains a length of 4.6 metres (15 feet). The heaviest rod-caught blue marlin weighed 624 kilograms (1,376 pounds). Its strength and power make it one of the hardest fish for anglers to reel in to the boat or shore.

Fastest sailor

The sailfish is probably the fastest swimmer in the ocean. It can race along in bursts of over 100 kilometres per hour (60 miles per hour). This beautiful fish, with its huge sail-like dorsal (back) fin, reaches 3.6 metres (12 feet) in length when fully grown. Other speedy swimmers are the wahoo, and the bluefin and yellowfin tunas, mentioned later.

A bite on the bottom

The six-gilled shark is a giant, at 6 metres (20 feet) long. This fish lives deep in tropical waters. Though it is lazy and inactive for much of the time, this streamlined and efficient hunter can catch bottom-living fish and crabs with an amazing dash of speed.

Tail-ender

The thresher shark is 6 metres (20 feet) long, but half of this is long, leathery, strap-like tail. It swishes the tail to herd shoals of fish into a tight group, when it can then swallow them.

Sometimes the thresher smashes its tail into the fish, to stun them.

The female thresher gives birth to about four babies, each 1.5 metres (5 feet) long.

Needle-fish

The houndfish is 1.5 metres (5 feet) long, and thin like a needle, with a narrow mouth full of tiny sharp teeth. It lurks near the surface of coastal waters all over the world, feeding on smaller fish. It seizes victims with its jaws and carefully flips them round, so that it can swallow them head-first.

Wolf in herring's clothes

The wolf-herring is a type of herring, but much bigger and fiercer. This great fish grows to 3.7 metres (12 feet) long and lives mainly in the Indian Ocean, just off the coast. Its smaller cousins, the ordinary herring, eat the tiny animals and plants of the plankton. But the wolf-herring is a swift hunter.

Feared, yet popular

The mako shark is dangerous and aggressive. It frightens and occasionally attacks people in the water. But it is also popular with anglers, because it puts up a brave fight when hooked and is difficult to bring in. The biggest mako ever caught by rod and line was a monster that weighed in at 505 kilograms (1,115 pounds), from Mauritius, Africa.

Fastest shark

The mako shark, at 4 metres (13 feet) long, is one of the fastest sharks in the sea. It needs to be, because it feeds on fast-swimming mackerel and tuna.

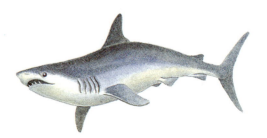

Not a mammal

The beautiful dolphinfish is another popular game fish. It is found in all warm seas, and although it looks like a dolphin (which is a mammal), it is a true fish, with its beautiful blue, green and yellow colouring. Female dolphinfishes are larger than the males, at about 1.5 metres (5 feet) long. They all fight powerfully when hooked.

They're playing our tuna!

The bluefin tuna (or tunny) grows to 4.5 metres (nealy 15 feet), and it weighs 800 kilograms (almost 1,800 pounds). It is the commonest of the tuna-fish group, and the most popular with sea anglers.

The biggest bluefin caught by rod and line weighed 679 kilograms (1,496 pounds).

Hooked by the giants

Game fish like the big sharks, marlins and tunas fight like fury when they are hooked. They leap, thrash, dive and dash, jerking the line and pulling the angler's boat many kilometres - even with the anchor down!

Be prepared

The game angler who hooks one of these monsters must be prepared. He or she is strapped into a special swivelling chair at the back of the boat. A lap pouch and straps hold the rod steady, so that the angler's arms aren't pulled out of their sockets!

The fight can go on for hours. The angler lets the line go out as the fish swims off, then reels it slowly back. In this way the fish gradually tires.

To catch a wahoo

The wahoo is another type of tuna, growing to 2 metres (6 feet, 6 inches) long. It is exceedingly fast - it has been timed at a speed of 77 kilometres per hour (48 miles per hour) in short bursts. It does this when it is chasing fish to eat - or when it is hooked by an angler.

How big is a bass?

The giant sea bass grows to 2.1 metres (7 feet) in length, and weighs more than 250 kilograms (550 pounds). It lives for a very long time, up to 75 years.

This formidable predator makes a good catch for the game angler. All bass are famed for their fighting power - and they are good to eat, too!

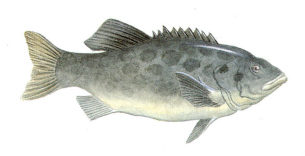

One egg, or two, or 12 million?

The tarpon is a big fish that looks rather like a giant herring. It is up to 2 metres (6 feet 6 inches) long and weighs 100 kilograms (220 pounds). It is covered with great silver scales, which are among the biggest of any fish. Tarpons do not breed until they are about 7 years old. After this, a female can produce 12 million eggs at a time.

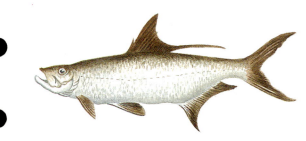

Sunfish . . .

Ocean sunfish are found in most seas except the cold waters near the poles.

These almost circular creatures cruise in the open ocean. In 1908, one got stuck in the propellor of a steamship in Australian waters. It measured 3.1 metres (10 feet) from front to back. It was also 4.3 metres (14 feet) from the tip of its upper fin to the tip of its lower fin. It weighed 2,235 kilograms (4,927 pounds).

. . . and Moonfish

Opahs or moonfish reach 1.5 metres (5 feet) in length and weigh 90 kilograms (200 pounds). They are a beautiful blue colour with bright red fins. Though they have no teeth, they are predators of mid-water fish and squid.

The biggest bony fish

Sunfish are the biggest (meaning heaviest) of the bony fishes. This is the group of fishes which have bony skeletons. It includes marlins, tunas, eels, barracudas, pike and similar fish. The sharks and rays belong to a separate group of fishes. They have a skeleton made of cartilage or gristle, not bone, and they are known as cartilaginous fish. There are far fewer members of this group, even though they grow bigger than bony fish.

Long and thin
The dealfish is related to the long oarfish. It has a red dorsal fin running along its long, thin body, from head to tail. Its tail fin turns upwards like a dainty fan. Although it looks streamlined, it is not an especially fast swimmer. The dealfish grows to 2.5 metres (8 feet) and feeds on fish and squid with its protruding mouth.

Rag rug
The brown ragfish would make a smelly hearth rug! It is a floppy fish which seems to be boneless, like a bundle of rags. It grows up to 2.1 metres (7 feet) in length and has no scales, spines or pelvic (rear) fins. Sperm whales like ragfish - not for hearth rugs, but for lunch!

Shipwreck home

The stonebass or wreckfish grows to 2 metres (6 feet 6 inches) and weighs 45 kilograms (100 pounds). It lurks deep on reefs, or even in shipwrecks, where it can hide and wait for small fish to swim near. Then it ambushes them.

What a mouthful

Porcupine fish have no need of speed. For defence, they are covered with spines, as their name suggests. The largest grows to about 90 centimetres (3 feet) long. It can inflate its body and make its spines stand out, to become as wide as it is long.

Giant rockpool fish

Try not to catch a wolf-fish in a rockpool! It is a type of blenny, but

instead of being finger-sized like the common blennies, the wolf-fish can be 2.5 metres (8 feet) long. It lives in the northern Pacific and Atlantic waters, feeding on starfish, crabs and sea urchins.

Caught by a carpet

The Australian wobbegong, or carpet shark, lies still on the sea bed, disguised as weeds and stones by its ragged frills and blotchy skin. This well-camouflaged brute, 2.5 metres (8 feet) long, suddenly opens its huge mouth and sucks in any unsuspecting fish or crab that has come too close.

Bottom notes

No prizes for guessing how the guitarfish got its name! This relative of the sawfish may be 3 metres (10 feet) in length.

Ugly but nice

The anglerfish grows to 1.8 metres (6 feet) long. Like the wobbegong, it sits on the sea bed. It sucks in any creature foolish enough to be attracted by its lure - a fin spine shaped like a rod and bait! Some people think its meat, known as monkfish, is delicious.

It swims slowly and grubs in the mud of shallow waters for shellfish and worms.

Do the conger!

Conger eels live all around Britain's coasts, hiding in rocky crevices and holes on the sea bottom. These local monsters can be 2.7 metres (almost 9 feet) long! They swim using the fin which runs from the head to the tail along their back, and back under the belly.

Eye-eye, sir!

Flatfish lie on one side of their body, on the sea bed. Most of them, such as flounders and plaice, lie on their right side and have both eyes on the left. But most halibuts have both their eyes on the right side of the head, and lie with the left side down.

The biggest flatfish

The halibut is probably the largest flatfish, growing to over 2 metres (almost 7 feet) in length and weighing up to 300 kilograms (660 pounds). It is a hunter with big teeth, and chases other fish far from the sea bottom.

A flat catch

The halibut is extremely difficult to pull up on a fishing line, since its wide body puts up great resistance.

The biggest halibut landed by rod and line was 161 kilograms (356 pounds), near Alaska in 1986.

Ratty tail

The strange ratfish can be 1.5 metres (5 feet) long, but a lot of this is its rat-like tail. It crunches up shellfish, starfish and sea urchins in deep Atlantic waters. It has a poisonous spine in its dorsal (back) fin, for self-defence.

All mouth and tail

Compared to its body size, the gulper eel must have the biggest mouth of any fish.

Gulp!

The gulper eel scoops up almost anything it can catch, in the blackness of the deep ocean. Its stomach is like a balloon that expands to hold fish much bigger than itself.

In fact, when it hasn't eaten for a time, it is just a mouth and a tail! At 2 metres (6 feet 6 inches) long, it is a giant among deep-sea fish, most of which are quite small.

Strange mates

Deep-sea anglerfish are different from their shallow-water cousins mentioned earlier. Females may reach 2 metres (6 feet 6 inches) when fully grown. Yet the males are tiny . .

Males grow on you!

A female deep-sea anglerfish could have trouble finding a mate in the vast darkness of the ocean deep. So she carries her mate with her. In fact, sometimes she carries several males, to make sure! The tiny males are only 15 centimetres (6 inches) long. They attach themselves to the female's much bigger body, and live off her like parasites.

The slimmer's-dream fish

Although the lancetfish grabs whatever it can catch, it never gets fat. It may be 1.8 metres (6 feet) long, yet it is so thin that it rarely weighs more than 0.5 kilograms (about 1 pound). It can fold its very tall dorsal (back) fin into a groove along its back, and it catches prey in its huge fang-filled mouth.

How big were prehistoric fish?

We know about prehistoric fish from their fossils (preserved bones and teeth). From the size of these, some prehistoric fish were huge, as explained here. But it's doubtful that any was bigger than today's record-holder, the whale shark.

The first fish

Fish first appeared in the seas over 500 million years ago. They were small creatures that would easily fit on your dinner plate. But they would make a tough meal - they had hard bony armour over their bodies. And they didn't have jaws or fins! They sucked up small bits of food from the bottom.

The first "Jaws"

Over the next 100 million years, the bones of the head and front gills of these early fish, turned into strong jaws. At last, fish could bite and chew and kill.

One of the biggest was Dunkleosteus, at 9 metres (30 feet) long. It was the largest animal in the whole world at the time. Its armour-plated head had hinges so that the great bony blades, lining its jaws like great teeth, could chop and chomp together.

Problems with fossil sharks

Sharks are very ancient - they were among the first fish in the seas. But their boneless, gristly skeletons did not make good fossils. So fossil experts have only their hard teeth to show how big they grew.

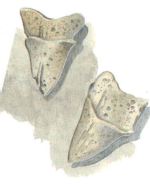

Prehistoric killers

One of these prehistoric sharks is known by its scientific name *Carcharodon megalodon*. It lived 15 million years ago, and it had teeth 15 centimetres (6 inches) long - bigger than a man's hand.

Some scientists used to think that, from the size of its teeth, this shark grew to 24 metres (80 feet) in length!

Not quite so big . . ?

However, some fish experts now believe that *Carcharodon megalodon* was probably nearer 13 metres (40 feet) long. So it was not quite as big as today's gentle whale shark. But it was a huge killer, like its descendant, the great white shark.

. . . Or was it?

There are a few fossilized teeth which could be from an even bigger *Carcharodon megalodon*, perhaps 15 metres (49 feet) in length. However, we cannot be sure, because the teeth in a shark's mouth vary in size from the middle to the side.

So, for the time being, it's safest to say that whale shark is probably the biggest fish that ever lived.

Big fish eats little fish

Xiphactinus was a large hunting fish, rather like a modern pike, but 4.3 metres (14 feet) long! The fossilized remains of this fish contain the bones of a smaller fish. This small victim was *Xiphactinus*' last meal, swallowed 100 million years ago.

A "lung" time ago!

Millions of years ago, fish and most other animals lived in the water.

Gradually some of the fish left the sea, to live on land. To do this, they had to develop lungs to breath air, and legs to walk on. They became amphibians.

Reminders of the past

Lungfish are true fish. But as their name suggests, they also have simple lungs, and they can breathe out of water for a time. Their fins are also like legs. The lungfish still surviving today may be similar to the first fish that came ashore, to crawl in the prehistoric ooze, more than 350 million years ago.

Biggest lungfish

The biggest lungfish today are 2 metres (6 feet 6 inches) long. They look similar to eels, and they live in the muddy swamps of Africa. Similar but smaller lungfish are found in South America and Australia.

When the swamps dry out, the lungfish may wriggle overland to a nearby river. Or it can bury itself deep in the mud and sleep until the swamp refills, at the next rainy season.

"Dinosaur" fish

Fossil experts once thought that another strange group of fishes, the "tassel-fins" or "lobe-fins", all died out 70 million years ago. This is the time when the dinosaurs began to disappear, too.
So when South African fisherman caught one of them - a living coelacanth - in 1938, it was like seeing a fossil that had come alive!

The amazing coelacanth

Coelacanths reach almost 2 metres (6 feet 6 inches) in length. They are very rare and found mainly near the Comoros Islands, in the Indian Ocean off Africa. Their fins have fleshy, muscular bases, and they can wave them around like arms or legs.

South American monster

The arapaima, also called the pirarucu, lives in the Amazon and Orinoco rivers of South America.

Many years ago, it may have grown to over 5 metres (16 feet) long and 200 kilograms (450 pounds) in weight. This would make it one of the biggest freshwater fish in the world. However most arapaimas today are much smaller. Reliable reports show that the biggest are probably 3 metres (10 feet) long.

Arapaima parent

The arapaima is a predator with a huge appetite. It is also a good parent. It makes a nest for its young and defends them fiercely. It can survive in swampy mud using its lung-like swim bladder to breathe air.

Teeth of the tiger

The giant tigerfish is a voracious predator in African lakes and rivers. At 1.8 metres (6 feet) in length, it can tackle fish just slightly smaller than itself.

The tigerfish has only a few teeth, but each one is large and very sharp. If an old tooth breaks off, a new one quickly grows to replace it.

Introduced peril

The great Nile perch, 2 metres (6 feet 6 inches) in length, has been introduced into many lakes and waterways, to provide much needed food for people living nearby. It has become one of the most important food fish in Africa. But there is a price to pay for the perch's success. As it feeds hungrily on the local fish, these are becoming rarer, and some may not survive.

Gentle giant

The mahaseer of Indian rivers feeds on small creatures and water plants. It is related to the goldfish, with a stout body and large scales. It is quite common and grows to about 1.8 metres (6 feet) long.

Estuary monster

The pa beuk is another contender for the world's biggest freshwater fish. However this giant catfish of South-East Asia lives also in the half-salty water in the estuaries (mouths) of big rivers such as the Mekong. So it is not a truly freshwater fish. Giants of 3 metres (10 feet) and 240 kilograms (530 pounds) used to be seen. But, like many other kinds of fish, the pa beuk is now rare and only smaller ones are caught.

Hoover fish

The pungas catfish is another big inhabitant of Asian rivers and estuaries. It only feeds at night, grovelling on the bottom to suck up rotting rubbish. Even on this diet, it attains a length of 1.2 metres (4 feet).

Wel, wel!

The European catfish or wels is another candidate for the biggest freshwater fish in the world. Monsters about 5 metres (16 feet) long, weighing 300 kilograms (660 pounds), were once said to live in rivers such as the Dneiper and Danube, in central Europe. But today they rarely live long enough to grow so huge.

The biggest wels

The largest accurately measured wels came from the River Danube. It was a female, 3 metres (9 feet 10 inches) in length.

Amazon giants

The thorny catfish or cuiu-cuiu is another South American giant, possibly up to 3 metres (10 feet) long. This fish lives at the bottom of the Amazon and Guyana rivers, sucking up rotting detritus with its toothless mouth.

Yet another catfish of this area is the lau-lau, which reaches 2.4 metres (8 feet) in length. And another is the pirahyba, of the Amazon, which can be 2.1 metres (7 feet) long and weigh 180 kilograms (almost 400 pounds).

Carp-hunting catfish

The wallago is a giant catfish of Asia, at 2 metres (6 feet 6 inches) in length. Unlike many other huge catfish, this one is a fierce predator, and its favourite food is carp.

The wallago waits for carp to migrate upstream in great shoals, to breed. Then it launches a frenzied attack, leaping out of the water and cramming as many carp as it can into its mouth.

The American record-holder

The biggest truly freshwater fish of North America is probably the alligator gar, of the Mississippi. Several of these giants have grown to almost 3 metres (10 feet) in length, and over 100 kilograms (220 pounds) in weight.

Canadian buffalo

The bigmouth buffalo is a fish of North American rivers and lakes. Like its hairy namesake on land, the buffalo or bison, this fish has a deep, heavy body.

The bigmouth buffalo feeds on small water creatures and grows to about 1 metre (3 feet 3 inches) long, when conditions are good.

Cat's whiskers

The blue catfish is another North American inhabitant.

At 1.5 metres (5 feet) in length, and 45 kilograms (100 pounds) in weight, it has few enemies - apart from humans. It finds its food of smaller fish and crayfish using its cat-like "whiskers" (barbels) to feel its way in the muddy water.

Upside-down swimmer

The Mekong catfish is yet another giant from South-East Asia. It has been known to reach 2.4 metres (8 feet) in length. Although it looks as though it is swimming upside-down, it is the right way up. This strange design helps it to grub about in the mud with its toothless mouth.

Down-under cod

The Murray cod, up to 2 metres (6 feet 6 inches) long and 100 kilograms (220 pounds) in weight, is Australia's largest freshwater fish. It has been introduced into canals and other man-made waterways, where it crunches up crawfish and small fish.

Not a cod

The Murray cod has a confusing name. It is not really a member of the cod group at all. It belongs to a fish group called the sea bass - yet it does not live in the sea, either! The "Murray" part of the name comes from the Murray River in south-east Australia, one of the main rivers where it lives.

Saw point

The strange sawfish sometimes strays into rivers, where it would be one of the biggest freshwater fish. But it is more usually found in shallow waters along the warmer sea coasts of the Atlantic and Indian Oceans. The sawfish can grow to 7 metres (23 feet) long, although a quarter of this is the saw. This has about 30 teeth along each side.

Slashed to death

The sawfish feeds by grubbing in the mud, disturbing buried shellfish and fish with its saw. Sometimes it swishes the saw about in a school of fish, killing and eating them. The sawfish can also slash its saw-teeth into any fisherman who catches it.

Mississippi paddler

The paddlefish lives in the River Mississippi. This 2-metre (6 feet-6 inch) beast has a huge spatula for a nose. It is related to the sturgeon, and it swims with its mouth open, filtering tiny creatures from the water for food.

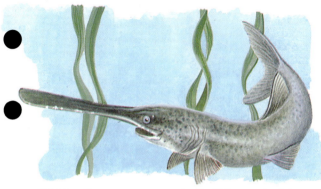

Hidden danger

The longnose gar lives in North American rivers.
The long nose is really its jaws, lined with sharp teeth. This sneaky fish hides its 1.5 metres (5 feet) of body in waterweeds, and shoots out to grab any fish that comes close.

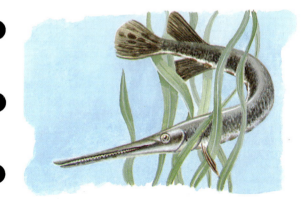

Britain's biggest

The largest freshwater fish in Britain is the pike. Like many other fish around the world, pike once lived to a great age, and grew much bigger in olden times. Today they are more likely to be caught by anglers in nets, or injured by a boat, or trapped by a weir, or suffer from pollution, before they grow old enough to become record-breaking giants of their kind.

Terror of the rivers

The pike is big, but stealthy and a master of disguise. It hides in waterweeds and catches smaller fish and other creatures, by darting out and grabbing them in its huge mouth, filled with sharp teeth. A big pike even attacks waterbirds, and small animals such as pet dogs that come to the water to drink. It drags them under until they drown.

"Freshwater Jaws"

The biggest pike were said to be over 40 kilograms in weight. Today 30 kilograms (67 pounds), and a length of 1.5 metres (5 feet), is considered exceptional.

The rod-and-line record for catching pike is 25 kilograms (55 pounds), for one caught in Germany. The British champion is a 20-kilogram (45-pound) pike from Wales.

Big, but not freshwater

Sturgeons also used to grow to gigantic size in olden days. Although these fish are often caught in rivers and lakes, they also live parts of their lives in the sea, so they are not truly freshwater.

Sturgeon records

The huge Russian sturgeon, known as the beluga, has supposedly been measured at 7.3 metres (24 feet) long and 1,474 kilograms (3,250 pounds) in weight.
Another type of sturgeon, the kaluga from north-east Asia, once reached more than 4 metres (13 feet) in length.

More sturgeon records

The white sturgeon of North America is a smaller kind of sturgeon. The scientifically-measured record is 3.81 metres (12 feet 6 inches) and 583 kilograms (1,285 pounds) in weight. The biggest rod-caught sturgeon of this type scaled 212 kilograms (468 pounds), in 1983.

The biggest common sturgeon from British lakes or rivers was trapped in nets in the River Severn, in 1937. Its length was 2.7 metres (nearly 9 feet) and it weighed 230 kilograms (507 pounds). A bigger common sturgeon, 3.18 metres (over 10 feet) in length and scaling 320 kilograms (705 pounds), was trawled from the sea near the Orkney Islands in 1956.

The biggest shock

Many fish use electric signals to help them find their way in murky water and to stun their prey. The most powerful fish-electricity is made by the South American electric eel. This creature weighs about 40 kilograms (88 pounds), is 2.5 metres (over 8 feet) long, and it can generate an electric shock of 650 volts - enough to kill a person!

A shocking stunner

When the electric eel is hungry, it hides near the muddy edge of the river, waiting for prey. It can even stun a cow or horse that comes to drink, from 6 metres (20 feet) away!

Electric knife

The Nile knifefish, 2 metres (6 feet 6 inches) in length, lives in the muddy shallows of the River Nile, in Africa. It uses its electric organ to find its way around, in the same way that a bat uses its ultrasound squeaks to navigate in the dark.

Rod-caught record

Alf Dean is a champion fisherman! In 1959 he caught a great white shark in South Australia. The giant weighed 1,208 kilograms (2,664 pounds) and measured 5.13 metres (16 feet 10 inches) long. It is probably the biggest fish ever caught on a rod and line.

Hooked chinook

The Pacific or chinook salmon is also very large, and the rod-and-line record is 44 kilograms (97 pounds). One caught in a net had a weight of 57 kilograms (126 pounds). That's the same as two average 9-year-old children!

The biggest price

The most valuable pet fish are koi carp. Koi are varieties of common carp that have been bred in captivity for many years. Their striking colours and patterns decorated ponds in peaceful Japanese gardens.

Big fish in little ponds

Koi grow to about 1 metre (3 feet 3 inches) long. To see their colours clearly, they need to be kept in small ponds or tanks but in very clean water, which is well-filtered.

Fish and chips

People all over the world eat lots of different types of fish. One of our most popular food fish is the cod. In the past, some cod weighed over 90 kilograms (200 pounds). But too much fishing has reduced their numbers and sizes. Today, cod rarely grow to more than 1 metre (3 feet 3 inches) long, and they weigh only about 20 kilograms (44 pounds).

One wing or two?

The skate is a relative of the shark, with a gristle (not bone) skeleton. It lives near the sea bottom, feeding on crabs lobsters and octopuses. A big skate is about 2.4 metres (8 feet) long and 1 metre (3 feet 3 inches) wide. Its eggs are known as mermaid's purses.

And a fishy tailpiece

The *smallest* fish in the world is the dwarf pygmy goby. It is only 10 millimetres (0.4 inches) long, and weighs just 5 milligrams (0.0002 ounces). It would take 6,000 of these fish to make one ordinary fishfinger! Dwarf pygmy gobies live in lakes and rivers of the Philippines.

Care for some caviare?

Caviare is a very expensive food delicacy, served in the best restaurants. In fact, it is the eggs from a female sturgeon fish. The largest sturgeons contain over 200 kilograms (450 pounds) of caviare.